## EARLY PRAISE FOR A COMPLICATED PIECE OF MACHINERY WITH NUMEROUS POSSIBILITIES FOR INJURY

"This inimitable book asks: How can we live organically in a world that seems to be falling apart? The speaker of these poems is challenged not only by personal history, but also by the physical environment in which this history takes place and challenges this personal history. Disasters, both natural and manmade, create a world on the precipice. This world out of balance is created vividly on the page. But more: this world is created with an energy that borders between destruction and resurrection, between chaos and joy. The book ultimately asks us to comb through our individual lives *and* the lives of the things, both animate and inanimate, that surround us. *A Complicated Piece of Machinery with Numerous Possibilities for Injury* introduces us to a poet who is, in a word, *necessary.*"

**KENNY FRIES**
award-winning author of *In the Province of the Gods*
and *In the Gardens of Japan*

"With a quiet wryness and quickening around what makes life electric, these poems are Maggie Cleveland's heirlooms. Whether through environs of the inner workings of elevators, landscape of Laurentide ice, or combusted relationships—that lost Victorian Prostitute Couch— whether in a series of erasures or wide-cast net of the book's final achievement, its long sequence centering a span of cosmic in cellular connections, the sensibility is always transporting and wise, her perambulations of mind admirably able to handle the understated as well as oracular. I particularly feel the way they 'take the weight of the loss and cast it against// what's left,' providing much care to notice."

**DOUGLAS A. MARTIN**

"William Carlos Williams once defined a poem as 'a small (or large) machine made of words,' and poet Maggie Cleveland's *A Complicated Piece of Machinery with Numerous Possibilities for Injury* memorably fleshes out that possibility by revealing that the heart itself is fabricated with switches and terminals, erotic charge and electrical voltage, plumb wires and infinite resistance. Separated into five sections—or floors— this book rises from an intimate look at the mechanics of elevators up through a series of compelling erasures of a public document on manufacturing accidents and finally onto the rooftop of a long poem that channels Charles Olson or Rachel Blau DuPlessis but that remains utterly distinctive in its evocation of an external and internal landscape perpetually decaying in time, where memory is a 'rough rope net' and our waters are 'almost safe for swimming.' Simultaneously canny with warning, structurally ambitious and deeply personal yet universal, Cleveland captures the scale, the tumult, the thrill and the quiet of contemporary life in a remarkable first book of poems."

**RAVI SHANKAR**
Pushcart Prize-winning author of 17 books

# A COMPLICATED PIECE OF MACHINERY WITH NUMEROUS POSSIBILITIES FOR INJURY

POETRY

MAGGIE CLEVELAND

A Complicated Piece of Machinery
with Numerous Possibilities for Injury

Copyright © 2024
Cover and book design by Andrew Keating

Paperback ISBN: 978-1-941462-29-4
eBook ISBN: 978-1-941462-30-0

Cobalt Press, a subsidiary of Cobalt Creative, LLC
Toledo, Oregon

cobaltreview.com
cobaltcreative.us

All rights reserved. No part of this book may be reproduced in any form, except for the inclusion of brief quotations in review, without written permission from the author/publisher.

For all inquiries, including requests for additional materials, please contact andrew@cobaltcreative.us.

# CONTENTS

## 1 ELEVATRIX

5    The Machinery of Beginnings
6    The Machinery of Wantonness
7    The Machinery of Modesty
8    The Machinery of Surprise
9    The Machinery of God Helping Those Who Help Themselves
10   The Machinery of Panic
11   The Machinery of Apology
12   The Machinery of Revision
13   The Machinery of Finding One's Bearings

## 2 THINGS I HAVE LEARNED

17   Things I have learned about elevators (words)
18   Things I have learned about elevators (need)
19   Things I have learned about elevators (fears)
20   Elevator Man's Love Song
21   Color Code for Resistors
22   Fifty 'Aught Miles: A Map

## 3 REPORTS OF ACCIDENTS

# CONTENTS

## 4 INVOLVING THE ENORMOUS

| | |
|---|---|
| 49 | Silence Goes Faster Backwards |
| 51 | Razing the Mills |
| 53 | On Melancholy and the Mystery of a Street |
| 54 | All of the birds in Vermont |
| 58 | Out from coastal fog |
| 59 | Before mid-morning slides to early afternoon |
| 60 | The blood around my heart |
| 61 | Overwintering |
| 62 | My body is concave, angular |
| 64 | Sing at the table |
| 65 | I didn't realize you were gone |
| 66 | Waking from a dream in which I was unsure if I were about to birth a child or a blueberry pie |
| 67 | Penumbra |
| 68 | we largely involve the enormous |

## 5 ATOM FISH

# A COMPLICATED PIECE OF MACHINERY WITH NUMEROUS POSSIBILITIES FOR INJURY

5   **ATOM FISH**

4   **INVOLVING THE ENORMOUS**

3   **REPORTS OF ACCIDENTS**

2   **THINGS I HAVE LEARNED**

1   **ELEVATRIX**

## THE MACHINERY OF BEGINNINGS

We will begin with the shunt field
winding. If the deflections

become larger, check
the voltage drop. Mark

the field wires, disconnect
them. Ensure the work

is plumb and square. Observe
the interpole windings, retract

at either or both limits of travel.
If motor shunt field current

drops, turn on the growler
and note the level of hum. Check

for unusual noise. Your meter
should read infinite resistance.

## THE MACHINERY OF WANTONNESS

You are surrounded by live
electrical equipment. As little
as .005 amperes of current

can be fatal. You must be aware
of electrical and mechanical
hazards, as well

as the danger of falling. During service,
it's often necessary to ride on top
of the elevator car. Chains

and sprockets can catch
loose clothing. You could become entangled
and injured, and have difficulty

getting free. Loose clothing
could twist between the hoist ropes
and the drive sheave of an elevator

machine. With power on,
the hazards are obvious. To prevent
damage to sensitive solid state

circuits, wear a grounding
wrist strap. Wear an insulated hard
hat and safety glasses. Stand

on a rubber mat. Be sure
your clothing and shoes are dry.

# THE MACHINERY OF MODESTY

Exposed electrical terminals are always waiting
for that careless moment. Worn gibs and sills can cause
problems, become flush with the commutator surface.
This involves a variety of factors, both mechanical
and electrical. If your diagnosis indicates that the motor
or generator needs to be disassembled, do not hammer
the end of the rosette into the shackle. The shock
will seat a properly made rosette.
Wear suitable protective equipment: a full face mask
with dark tinted glass. Leather chaps are recommended.
Wear a safety shield to protect your eyes. If the deflections
become larger, twist the two ends of the wire together.
The condition usually continues to worsen until remedied.
An observant mechanic can take action before serious trouble occurs.

## THE MACHINERY OF SURPRISE

When the car
is traveling toward
the top of the hoistway,

the counterweight
is plunging downward
toward the pit

without making
a sound.

# THE MACHINERY OF GOD HELPING THOSE WHO HELP THEMSELVES

You usually don't have to worry
about a passenger elevator door
falling on you. If the upper door panel

gets jammed or stuck in the open
position, it is extremely dangerous, even
with the main switch pulled. If the stuck

section suddenly becomes free, the panel will fall
like a guillotine. Anything in its path
will be crushed or severed. Never stick

your head in between the upper
and lower panel to see what's wrong. Block
the doors open securely to be certain

they won't fall before proceeding. Safety
must be your number one concern at all times.

## THE MACHINERY OF PANIC

The overloads
have tripped.

The loop
circuit is open.

A warning bell
is required.

A void can allow the anchor
to shoot straight through
like a bullet. Avoid

being splashed by blood.

## THE MACHINERY OF APOLOGY

You cannot use a false car to hoist doors
from floor to floor. The tension device needs to move freely
with the brush as it follows irregularities. Molten babbitt
can cause water to flash into steam and spew babbitt. A
sleeve bearing quietly wears. Such conditions result
in fractured brushes, vibration due
to imbalance. Tension on brace rods
will cause excess stress on stiles.
The problem may be corrected by turning
and undercutting. Retract at either or both
limits of travel. If motor shunt field current drops,
a relating device is required.
All of the material remaining after this operation
must be carefully vacuumed away.

## THE MACHINERY OF REVISION

Drop 2 plumb wires from as high
as possible down to pit. Be certain
wires are clear of obstructions
all the way down.

Use heavy plumb weights; be sure
they've stopped moving before
starting measurements. To adjust
to uneven surfaces, use leveling jacks

instead of blocking. Do not force
braces to fit. Level the scaffold
until proper fit can be easily
achieved. Fasten braces securely.

Watch out for obstructions and holes
in the floor. Use capstan or winch,
attached to truck bed, to prevent
free-wheeling. Mouse the hook
of the hoisting block or well wheel.

Try not to work with a meter lead
in each hand. Use care not to over-torque.

## THE MACHINERY OF FINDING ONE'S BEARINGS

Never make an adjustment until you know
why you are making it and how it is
to be made. Never change brushes
on rotating equipment until the power
is turned off and the equipment
is no longer moving. Never work
on a live circuit while standing
on metal work in water. Continuously
observe power-on conditions.
The answer to two questions will generally give
you the information you need to decide
what the problem is. The questions are:
What is the elevator not doing that it should be doing?
What is the elevator doing that it should not be doing?

5 ATOM FISH

4 INVOLVING THE ENORMOUS

3 REPORTS OF ACCIDENTS

2 THINGS I HAVE LEARNED

1 ELEVATRIX

## THINGS I HAVE LEARNED ABOUT ELEVATORS (NEED)

Picture New York without elevators—

squat buildings, fat business-
men climbing stairs to sweat
in their suits, damp handkerchiefs
brought forth to wipe exertion
from the face—

      what capital could bloom
so distant from the sun?

what industry could breed beneath
such low ceilings?

## THINGS I HAVE LEARNED ABOUT ELEVATORS (WORDS)

elevator, dumb-
waiter, man-lift
funicular, APM

a lifting device
made of cables, electrically
charged to drive traction

& counterweight
systems, hoist
people or things—

or power a pump for hydraulic
oil, raising a plate on
a piston (a jack)

by type, a vertical
transport system equipped
to move people

or goods between floors
of a building,

a cage and its machinery,
housed in a shaft—

a platform, a room
to carry, to raise,

conveying objects or ideals
to different levels—

## THINGS I HAVE LEARNED ABOUT ELEVATORS (FEARS)

Don't worry about the cable snapping, car plummeting
through a dark and empty shaft to crash spectacularly
on the basement floor. In very tall buildings,
the elevator's roped with at least six cables
spun of steel—or—in a building of fewer floors, shuttled back
and forth by a column of pressurized oil. Roped traction machines
are equipped with an overspeed governor to monitor irregularities
in speed. Should it exceed its predetermined rate of floors
per minute, the wedge brake will engage
to stop the car immediately—a starling and unpleasant jolt
for the rider, but superior to its alternative.
Only if cables are severed by an outside force (re: 9/11)
will such a downward plunging catastrophe occur.

## ELEVATOR MAN'S LOVE SONG

Plumbed the jack an hour before first light. By afternoon
the heat had dulled the buzz of the machine room, till
a ruptured valve blew everything to hell. The crew won't split
until it's fixed, each corner squared, each measurement
precise. Drove home again at 3AM. The night road pulsed
behind my eyes. My blood's been transubstantiated,
all that's fluid beats hydraulic oil. What's left to love of this,
beyond the twisted back, the ridged knees wracked
from hours spent knelt on escalator steps? All solace here
is gathered where it lives: from wife & child ensconced at home,
to night-shift clerk or waitress kindnesses, to oath, to obligation sworn
to trade, to brother, crook of the arm to fist.

# COLOR CODE FOR RESISTORS

Did you hear the one etched deep in ceramic, hid
in a series of rainbow bands? A joke splicing rape
with a racist jab; a dig at a woman who wanted
to fuck like a man. There are rules for resistance.
Electrical current flows through a circuit like water
flows through pipe, like blood through veins. The force
that sets it in motion is voltage. Resistance controls
the flow in the way that a dam slows a flood to a trickle.

Your sister Violet is riding her bike to work. The street
is the circuit; the voltage, the push of her feet on the pedals.
She coasts down the hill like current over the road. When men
on the sidewalk impede her path, what more can we expect of them

when what they've been told is though it takes some wrangling,
once you pin her down, Violet gives willingly. Get some now.

## FIFTY 'AUGHT MILES: A MAP

If you are awake,   head west and over the bridge. If the bridge   is open—open to boats—it'll take   20 minutes. Turn   your ignition off. If the weather's too cold,   the gears will freeze. You'll be out   of luck. If it's humid,   the joints   will swell. Either way,   it'll stick. If it's stuck, the cops   will arrive to shoo the cars away. If it's not, wait   for the gates to swing up, and drive.

Don't lose your breath   in the dead-fish smell. On the side,   they drop bait   onto lobster boats, and mackerel that has just begun to rot   works best. In the   summer, the odors settle   around the city. You'll never mistake   low tide. On second thought,

you might rather meet me at work. Take a right at the sign   INDUSTRIAL PARK. Drive past the gym/   megachurch and the Firearms School.   The road will curve   for a bit. Take a right   at the stop sign, and look   to your right again.

People ask about the INDUSTRIAL PARK   where I work; it's the one   where the football   player shot the other football player   in the middle of the night. I wasn't work   -ing when it happened, but third-shifters   the next building over heard the bangs. I was sleep   -ing

fifty-aught miles away   at home. They slept   while I drove by the death spot   twice a day for three days till they found   the body. The lot where they shot him

isn't entirely empty. Bulldozers pushed   the sandy soil to 20-foot dunes not unlike the seashore   in places, left ragged   brush to push back   through the ground. In years, a forest   may grow back, though shorter/ sparser; (maybe) enough   to cover a body tossed on a path   in a landlocked INDUSTRIAL PARK.

I live blocks   from the ocean, across   from a football field on Route 6. The player who died   in the dunes had surely played   on a high school field   when he was young, in a warmer   climate. All football players come from the south. The local kids play   on the field   across Green Street. We come   from the northeast.

When I'm lying in bed on the week    -ends, I listen to    the announcer man.
I don't have so much energy    myself. This isn't new,    but I'm older, it's
worse.

When I was young, I snuck into the athletic supply shed in the field. The shed
    was knocked down. There's a new    supply    shed now, with a
lock. The kids can't sneak in    anymore. The boy I snuck in with    grew
up. We're friends now, on Facebook. I see him    in the supermarket, I
pretend    that I don't. I grew up to work    in an INDUSTRIAL PARK.
I still like    poems.

    In the later    *Maximus* poems, Charles Olson turned    maps into poems,
layering poems over poems,    bound by Gloucester,    the Greeks,
    and cartography. Though I'm neither    man nor philosopher, I

can read maps. Fairhaven is fifty-aught miles    south of Gloucester. You drive
there, you'll put more    than fifty miles on your engine. There are
no direct roads    linking the two. In

'The Perfect Storm,' Sebastian Junger    said, "If Gloucester is the delinquent kid
    who's had a few scrapes    with the law, New Bedford's the truly    mean
older brother who's going to kill    someone one day." I don't think he spent much
time

    in New Bedford, the city a'one aught-mile    over the bridge. I don't
think he spent much time    with my stepfather, either, though quoting him:
"The vessel is well suited    for its purpose. Submitted without
    prejudice, David    C. DuBois."

I would guess    that the quoted report was written at what's now
my kitchen table. I bought    his house and the table, too, eventually.
I almost forgot    about the map. Your map. I could argue there's pieces of it
    in 'The Perfect Storm,' but that's kind    of a stretch.

    If after all of this, you still    want the map but you are,    in fact, sleeping, I'd
give
    you the same directions I'd give    you if you were awake, but I'd caution
        that when you arrived you

may not be the same    person you'd been when you made    the request.
When you crossed

the threshold, your fingers had changed. You'd look more     like my cousin, a lady I used
          to work with, but wearing     her brother's empty thighs
as your arms. Or your face would be the same,      but you'd have the eyes
          from his dog. When you entered

the house, the living     room would be from the house   I lived in in '96. Or your own     house, if your house were mine. Not just that—

          I'd be splayed          on the Victorian Prostitute Couch my former
sister-in-law's ex-   husband chopped up with an axe and threw in the fire
          after    their divorce. I feel like I'm lying     when I tell you this
because I am. There was no axe. There was no fire. There was a sister
          in law. We divorced

(though I married      again. And divorced again, too). She's one of the
things I lost      in the split. There was also     a couch, but who knows
          what happened. Maybe her ex-   husband or my ex-    husband used it
          to start     a fire

          —the map. You'd find it

but not in the room
you were looking for—that room
has disappeared. You'll give up,

get back     in your car, and head west      on Route 6. It's not on the hour
     or a quarter-after; the bridge     is not open
this time. You will drive      across in a minute flat, looking back

at the boats and the football field—

          they'll disappear. You'll bear right
at the dry ice processing    plant, and on to

the solid highway, on which
you'd be sure
                    you were no
longer sleeping.

5 ATOM FISH

4 INVOLVING THE ENORMOUS

3 REPORTS OF ACCIDENTS

2 THINGS I HAVE LEARNED

1 ELEVATRIX

# REPORTS OF ACCIDENTS.

## REPORTS OF ACCIDENTS IN MANUFACTURING AND MERCANTILE ESTABLISHMENTS.

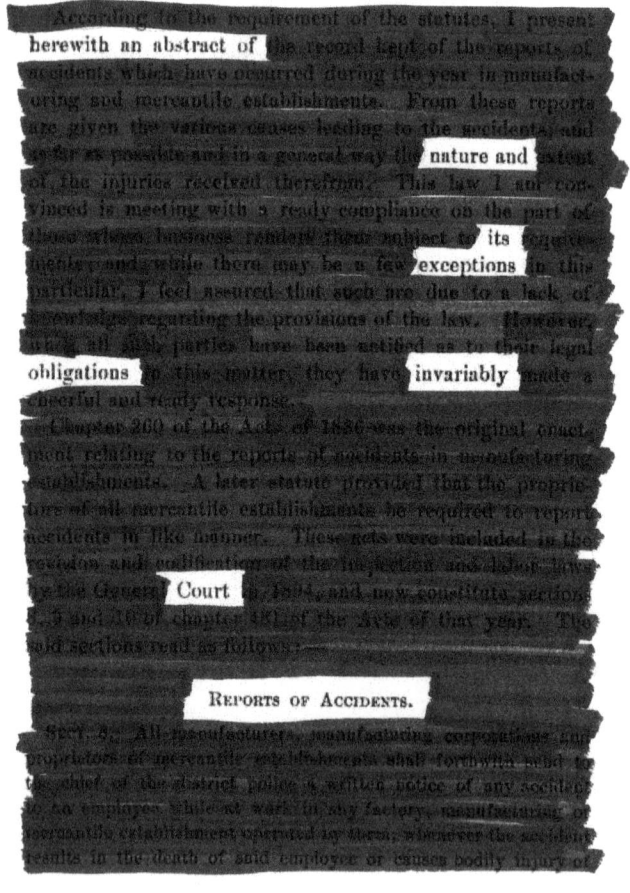

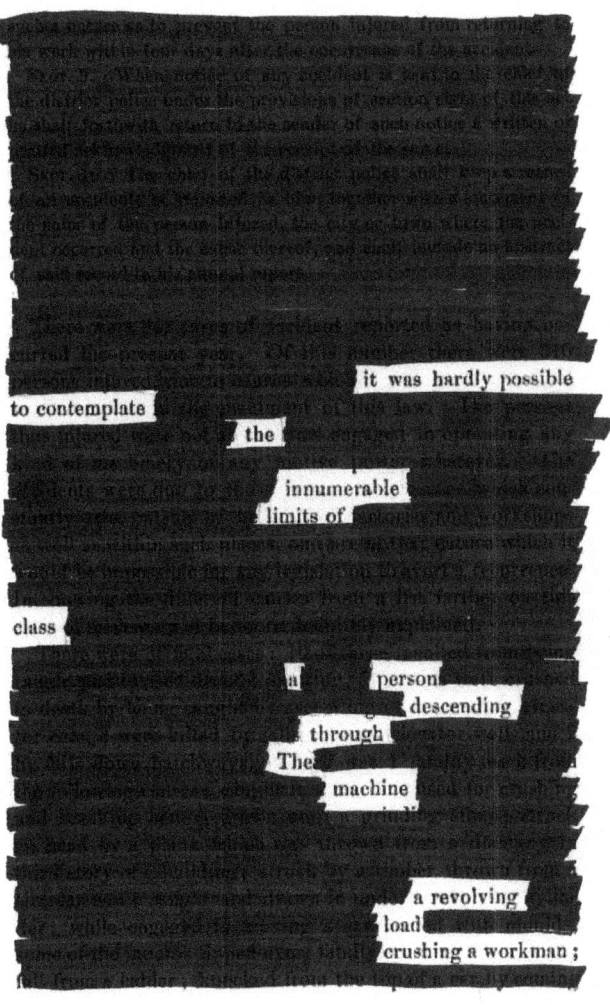

it was hardly possible to contemplate the innumerable limits of class a person descending through The machine a revolving load crushing a workman;

# A COMPLICATED PIECE OF MACHINERY

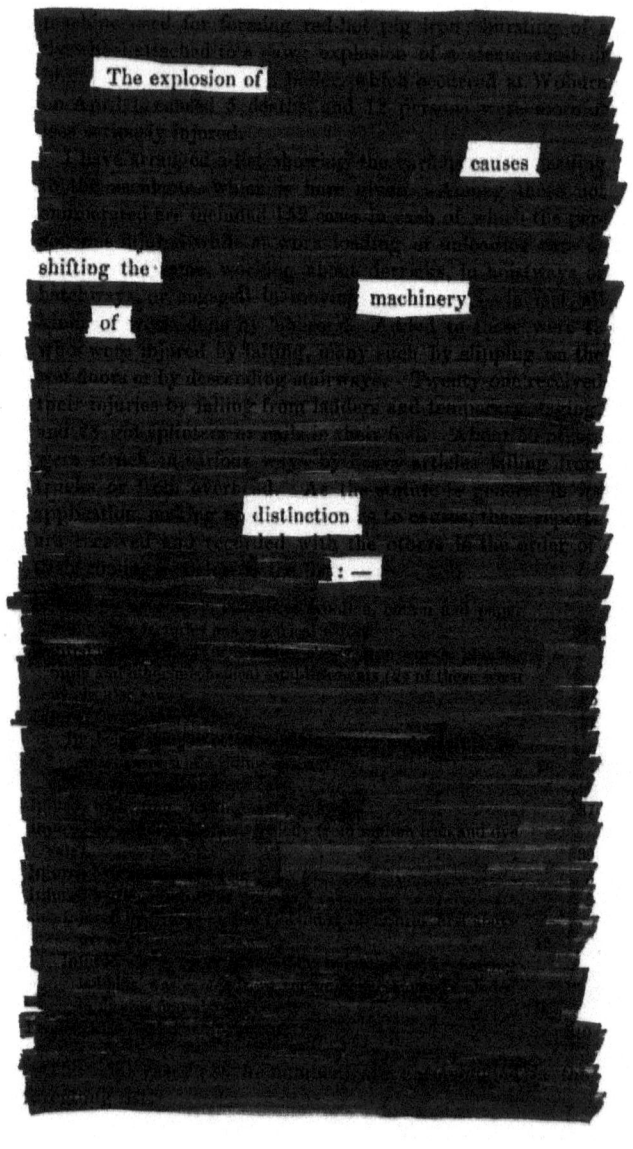

The explosion of causes shifting the machinery of distinction

402 REPORT CHIEF OF DISTRICT POLICE. [Jan.

*attempting motion, we become entangled in the running machine* a large proportion suffer their own thoughtless acts each lost to a slight of the body

1896.] PUBLIC DOCUMENT — No. 32. 403

caught between the brickwork and the flesh his body an operative of fatal establishment

404 REPORT CHIEF OF DISTRICT POLICE. [Jan.

the

break   crushing
                the

weak    and fallen

It is supposed    he lost his balance
making the shift.

No one witnessed the

empty case
                        ascending
instantaneous,          no sound.

1896.] PUBLIC DOCUMENT — No. 32. 405

the influence of
sleep
rolled off the
darkness

he

refused,
The urge
insisted
a
rushing

River
passing
through
the body

# A COMPLICATED PIECE OF MACHINERY

While engaged in
the immediate
his hook slipped off
the frame
all
The
years
rough castings for
the machine

408 REPORT CHIEF OF DISTRICT POLICE. [Jun.

morning

knew nothing about the working of
desire

leaning over
the well,

One of the workmen

was caught

# A COMPLICATED PIECE OF MACHINERY

410  REPORT CHIEF OF DISTRICT POLICE. [Jan.

412 REPORT CHIEF OF DISTRICT POLICE. [Jan.

with bare hands he took the full force of the current travelling towards the smoke from the burning bridge thrown over around the fly wheel, thrown over the same bones the pawl and ratchet

# A COMPLICATED PIECE OF MACHINERY

1896.] PUBLIC DOCUMENT — No. 32. 413

in

These
ribs,

throttled
pressure

set to blow

leaving the machinist
to commence

the
withrawal of

work

414 REPORT CHIEF DISTRICT POLICE. [Jan. '96.

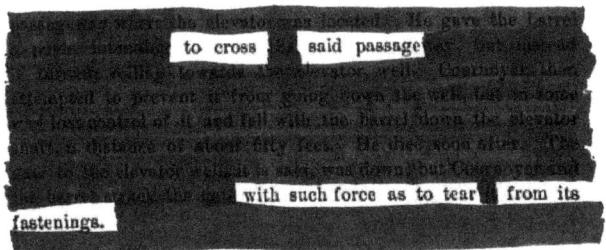

5 ATOM FISH

4 INVOLVING THE ENORMOUS

3 REPORTS OF ACCIDENTS

2 THINGS I HAVE LEARNED

1 ELEVATRIX

## SILENCE GOES FASTER BACKWARDS

It starts with abandoned textile mills that rose
in crumbling brick façade, hung over
the toxic river. Make of that what you will.

Of course, there's an elevator—the rickety kind
with the gate you close yourself, like the one
I rode with my grandfather up to his brother's

printing shop. Another one—dead relatives,
a few of those, who're sometimes / sometimes not
cognizant of the metaphysical warp they've endured.

Eventually, I'll remember it for them, just before
I wake up. (There I go again, confounding dreams
with poems.) Don't worry about the form, the letters

drop into that themselves. There'll be some shuffling
down the line. And then—the arrival of those
insipid birds, black crows or starlings, magpies

heckling from rafters, snapping their beaks on bits
of my old mythologies, nothing important
to say. Who cares, until they see themselves

the blight spread out like oil spilled west
from failed New England cotton towns across
the land, each bulldozed field upending

shuttered shopping malls / conveyances within,
unearthing coffins of their own dead relatives
from less than final rests. Open the lid, and thrust

your hand down deep to the dense core center,
pit o' the peach. Start from the middle, build up
and down concurrently, above/below till it puffs

and swells like the breast of a fledgling wren
(I told you they'd get back in). At the end,
you stand in an empty room, unsure

of what to say. You stammer a bit, give up,
stomp out and kill the lights. When the door
slams shut behind you, there's nothing but silence.

After a while, the walls begin to speak.

## RAZING THE MILLS

The wrecking ball
like a clumsy metronome
keeps time
in staggered beats
as it taps
the façade
of the monolith
with a heavy
kiss.

Asbestos laden
frames crack,
panes of glass and
floorboards steeped in
a hundred years of machine oil
and sweat
split,

tumble down the bones
of the behemoth,
slam the ground
and send a rumble
to the rocks
across the river.

What's left is blasted to bits -
bulldozed, swept
into tall piles,
shoveled into trucks
and hauled away,

or blown by handfuls
into the wind
with a wish

that they won't
fill the hole
with poison this time,
that what's built

in its flattened place
won't be an empty box
of concrete and glass
with a sun bleached
"for lease"
sign in the window—

this year, the air
is tinged in color,

even the tips
of the seagulls' wings
are red.

## ON MELANCHOLY AND THE MYSTERY OF A STREET

>   *Et quid amabo nisi quod aenigma est?*
>   (an inscription by Giorgio de Chirico on a self-portrait, 1911)

The wagon
is empty. The birds
have gone mute.
The tigers have left
for home.
A mistake, I'd concede,
seeing only around
the corner impending doom.
An equal mistake—
seeing only the street's stone doors
in diminishing gloom.

As if the hoop could spin of its own accord—

all tricks
of the light, love's reverse projection
of objects in space,
the impetuous reach
      of shadows cohering in form—
the girl's unstoppable approach,

each whack of metal on wood
sending shocks through her hands
till they're numbed
enough to forget
they are clutching the stick.

## ALL OF THE BIRDS IN VERMONT

All of the birds in Vermont are black,
except for the birds that aren't black.

Hawks circle tops
of trees, tracking movements
& heat—
the precipice springs up,
becomes the view.

\*

All of the birds in Vermont are black,
except for the birds that are brown.

I met him in a concrete well
at the top of a hill.
Our discourse was
thicker than trees, fraught with leaves,
didn't question
how it came to be
that the year's first frost killed off
the mosquitoes
as the Cardinal's egg cracked
in the spring.

\*

All of the birds in Vermont are black
except for the birds that are red.

The trick's
in distinguishing movement
from absence of movement;

in seeing in stillness
the cycling/recycling of breath,

recognizing a cloud's mass
of autonomous drops
as a frozen lake stuck in the sky
that would crash to the earth

if it weren't so goddamn sure
it could do it alone.

\*

All of the birds in Vermont are black
except for the birds that are gray.

In each clump of dirt
that is stuck to our shoes

there are 2,000 years of sediment
scraped from permineralized rock,
pushed up by a frozen comb
carving lines in the ground,
bearing down southeast.

In the early morning
I dug my car out
from the snow
with raw hands,
kicked ice
from my tires

my lungs and then my whole body burned
as I scurried away
to meet him
in the city.

\*

All of the birds in Vermont are black
except for the birds that aren't birds.

Once there was a man
who refused to be entombed in ice

so he ripped himself
from the land, bought a ticket
to a place where it never snows.

The water leeched
out of his body,
his voice dried up
like an old leaf.

I brushed the shriveled pieces
from my hair.

\*


All of the birds in Vermont are black
except for the birds that are white.

A flash of being charged
split
the moment: the deer
leapt in
        to the woods.

A sight I might have missed
had I not been roused at 3AM
to descend scuffed stairs, crouch
on a rough four-inch stoop,

lean back to look
at a sky of aging light,

relearn a land I loved,
which hadn't changed.

\*


None of the birds in Vermont are black
except for the birds that are black.

They coast over
striated rocks left scattered
by Laurentide ice.

I split from a life
that won't fit.

The pond cracks
like a shotgun

water rushes up
the side of the mountain

sap courses
down the tree

the sugared
blossoms of spring

sweeten the ground
for those whose shoes

are caked
with our dust.

## OUT FROM COASTAL FOG

the inland trees are breathed
back into color. Geese
tumble clumsily to sky,

beat black wings back
against the air.

Miles from shore,
the sky's the glistened gray
of scallop's maw

whose shell is larger
than my palm,

whose mollusk flesh
will split away from dawn,

*the knife's quick sweep—*

## BEFORE MID-MORNING SLIDES TO EARLY AFTERNOON

I have to speak of the sun on my skin, how I bared it and lay
on a plastic mat in the sand, listening to talk of oil extracted

from under the earth's tectonic plates. We've been sucking it up
from its cushioning wells, he said, and it's this that will lead

to our end. I thought - what does it matter, all of the damage
we've done – the earth will be good to get rid of us. Once we're gone,

the wells will replenish themselves. Later that day riding home, the highway
wind nearly knocked me off the scooter. Hot air blasted my face so hard

it began to lose feeling. I thought – how good it is to feel at all, given
last week's ruminations on walking into the ocean, car tumbling off

the bridge to the black surf below. All that was lost – this is what makes it
come back: the brief exchange with recklessness, my body pressing

against the wind to see which of us is more stubborn. Relativity posits
that gravity's not a force of its own but a consequence of imbalance;

one more trick of the awful rowing toward stasis. Once this is understood,
it's easy enough to correct: take the weight of the loss and cast it against

what's left. The sun will continue to burn my skin from millions of miles away.
I'm the fool at the edge of the Anthropocene, laying here, offering it up.

# THE BLOOD AROUND MY HEART

was roiling too, my heart a red siphonophore
flicking its man-o-war limbs in my chest.
The ocean's green-blue molecules grayed, undulating
like mercury cupped in my palm. I flipped
to my stomach, exposing my back to the sun
while the sea's surface churned. Too late
in the season for swimming, I clenched
hot fistfuls of sand for their warmth.

A month before, I floated just yards from here—
my arms barely needing to flutter
to keep me upright, my back to the noises
onshore, directing my sight to a vista
outside of time—a hundred-year bend
of light sand bordered by evergreens, sky
full of cumulus clouds spilling over themselves,
wind moving through me like it was a tongue
and I was a hole where a tooth had been pulled.
Beside me the jellyfish bobbed, their slippery
ovoid bodies bumping my arms and legs.
The sea wants none of me today, so I stay
on the blanket, thinking of all of the things I've done
wrong, slapping the green-headed horseflies
trying to needle a mouthful of blood for their eggs.
The curve of the earth fades sideways into the sky
and comes up empty. Everyone's left, I'm alone
on the sand shouting foolish questions
into the wind. How many times will it take you
to learn it. Look at the indifference of the sea.

## MY BODY IS CONCAVE, ANGULAR

children fill in
the spaces, curling up like little foxes
with sharp claws

to rest
in the hollowed out
earth

# OVERWINTERING

Morning. With a song
at 4AM, the babies fall from trees.

Robins tug worms
from the lawn, culling crumbs
tossed from the window
the night before.
Sparrows fly back to their eaves
in the old garage.

I hoist the door up on its hinge
with a clank. The walls
inside the garage are black,
flake easy where fire climbed
until I ran to grab the hose
to spray it down.

I want to believe the birds
remember nothing, not

the slap-black thunder, not
the lightning's quick
retaliatory flame, the heat,
or how their home
was gone.

All winter, the ones who stayed
dragged scraps
of singed chaff over the grass,
tugged clumps
of rabbit fur from brambles,

foraged scraps
to build new nests
from the wreckage
of the old.

When spring comes back,
I'll pull my daughters' bikes
from the pile where they've lain
since the storm,

wipe soot from the frames,
fill the tires, oil the chains—

and we'll ride
in crooked lines
down to the beach,

charred feathers
thrumming in our spokes.

## SING AT THE TABLE

Squeezing a rill of water
from my hair, my fingers closed
on something sharp. My hands

shook out the drops. Dark clumps
of feathers fell. I stuffed them
down the drain & dressed for work.

On the highway, I could hear
a throaty caw. I rolled
the window up, spun back the black
rock volume knob & followed
his directions to my door.

Dinner came to pass. I hung my head
above spaghetti. Near my ear, a beak
poked out, sucked up a noodle whole.

He paused to hand me a napkin.
I chewed it like bread.

## I DIDN'T REALIZE YOU WERE GONE

till you returned. The bloomed trees shook. The dog threw herself
at an 8-foot fence, frightening strangers on their way to the beach. I walked
until my pen ran out. Daffodils nodded their mute bud heads. I'm not
as friendly as I used to be. Birdbaths shaped like tulips
ate the tulips. A stone cracked into the shape of an upside-down
heart. The words so slow in coming I might as well walk into the ocean like my ex

after the Zoloft kicked in and he didn't want to be touched. Mute like a flower,
mute like a songbird stuffed, I turn to what I've forgotten:
the street, just blocks from home - the church where I was married,
its steps. The mute saints nod their heads. They're not as friendly
as they used to be. I ran until my pen walked out, my heart cracked
into the shape of an upside down stone. Tulips shaped like birdbaths
had been birdbaths all along. I didn't realize you'd returned till you were gone.

## WAKING FROM A DREAM IN WHICH I WAS UNSURE IF I WERE ABOUT TO BIRTH A CHILD OR A BLUEBERRY PIE

If a child, then no,
it's too much. But a pie
would be fine.

## PENUMBRA

After an hour a hand
reaches up and shakes the core

tip of the mind tilts
to catch & absorb

the words floating
above your skin. We've

known each other only
in warbling light, no cover
of darkness, no pretense

only my body shaking above you,
its blurred edge lit as we turn

from backs to curled sides, heads
propped up on our arms, hands

tracing curves of cheekbones, chins

& waiting to see what time
will make of us, all the rest

obscured.

## WE LARGELY INVOLVE THE ENORMOUS

we largely involve the enormous,
obstruct
a designated language
for its own sake

we sensationally
noisy sheep
up a mountain, an
inexcusable tangle
of rods & weaves -

this wilderness
possessing meaning,

imperceptibly
passing over grass,

roughly throwing
its newborn language—

information
shorn to words

gives birth
to the end
of the book

5 ATOM FISH

4 INVOLVING THE ENORMOUS

3 REPORTS OF ACCIDENTS

2 THINGS I HAVE LEARNED

1 ELEVATRIX

# ATOM FISH

**Prologue**


Aspects:
opposites.

Invisible from where I sit,
you insist
these happenings
 are real, their
odd combinations
can create anything—

china doll,
oak tree, elephant,
fish—

red banana,

beetles,
jasmine rice—

a blue orb
swirled with white—

**1.**

*NEW YORK, Aug. 17 – (AP) –*
*Hydrogen bombs are sometimes called atomic fish,*
*while atom bombs are atomic matches. The atomic fish*
*are the particles which form all atoms.*

*There are only three particles – neutrons, protons, and electrons.*
*Two or more of them get together to form any atom.*

On my dirty harbor beach
a half mile
from the sewage treatment plant,
a mile from the Superfund
river that
   flows through

it is almost safe
for swimming.

They want
to build a river walk
and a boat house—

(fine if you don't fall in)

Not
like when I was five, we all thought nothing
of bathing in a soup of laughter and PCBs
at East & West Beach

Not
like when my father was a kid
and jumped into the muck hole
at Sullivan's Ledge
to save the poor dog
who fell in
      to the quarry—

It was a sunny day.

Adam

in the guise of
a slippery fish

flopped up on the dock
near the boats
and waited to die.

**2.**

> *Why are they like fish? Because they change weight,*
> *like fish in or out of water. A fisherman never weighs his catch*
> *under water, where the buoyance would cut the weight.*

Memory:
a rough rope net,

hands reeking of diesel,
buckets of brine,
salt air—

the bent ends
of cigarettes pushed down
in brown sand.

A car barrels
over the causeway. Under black
water, silver gills

                glint.

3.

> *The three atomic particles act just like the fish.*
> *They weigh less after they enter the nucleus*
> *of an atom than when they are outside.*

Is it that my eyes are older
or that I've grown
more of them?

Was it me who changed,

or did the sea floor
    turn inside-out,

the water become the air, the sheen
of purple green oil
glistening on the surface
of the harbor,
on the cilia
    of our lungs?

Atom Fish:
when you shed
your heavy scales,
slipped through
the meniscus

did the mercury in your belly
float or sink?

4.

> *The loss of mass when these particles join up
> in atoms makes the H-bomb. The mass they lose
> in forming helium turns mostly into heat. This heat
> may be hotter even than the centers of stars.*

On land, one generation removed
from child-uncles crouched
under desks when alarm bells rang,

we were
        the last of those
who scanned the ground for shelter
when the planes flew overhead,

who giggling,
        scuttled by
fallout signs
        they'd nailed
to the doors of our schools, our

voices hollow and pale,
lighter than air,

        the first
        to take for granted a legacy
that could sear us
        with the heat
of stars.

5.

*The reason for the lost atomic mass is not buoyancy.*
*The mass is given up because it isn't needed.*


these things I've rejected, the things
from which I've turned my
head by a kitchen
stove, spit a word, walked
away—

\*

After an old stone bank, an alley
swept warm with exhaust,
        is a building of
gray white brick, its windows
smoke smudged.

        My mother worked
on Saturdays. In a square
city church, I knelt
with a bowed head.

The clank of thurible against chain
swilled through the air
with smoke.

        Grandmother's links of silver
circled through her fingers,
counting out novenas
to the patron saint
of lost causes.

At six, I lingered
near the chapel's edge, transfixed
by a dead child saint, candles
at her feet. With a dime
in a slot, I'd touch a lit stick
to the wick, crush
its brittle tip
in a cup of sand,
make a wish.

On the altar,
a locked golden box, a
chalice engraved
with a fish.

**6.**

*The loss is replaced by a force inside the atomic nucleus,*
*which grabs the new particles and holds them tight.*

Knob-knitted seaweed
sweater, smooth rock
underwater. A yellow rope's
burned off end
dipped in glue. My hands

count my children
to make sure
they're tangible—
it's enough
to keep me awake.

Adam Fish,
are we in this together?

Atom Fish,
am I in this alone?

7.

> *This mysterious force is a binding energy*
> *which seems to be the most powerful thing*
> *in the universe. It exists only inside atomic nuclei.*

The midwife said reach down
and pull her out.
It was early morning, the sky
that deepest blue
      before the sun.

Under a spotlight
I lifted her up by her arms.
      She was plopped
on my belly, a
wiggling, slippery
fish, thin skin,
and quick black eyes that
           blinked—

cleaned of her scales,
she was numbered,
wrapped, and weighed.

They snapped a bracelet
on my wrist, passed
me a compact little being.

We passed into
a sightless
world. We learned
to breathe water.
We slept.

When I woke,
our gills had closed.

I stood. I carried
my daughters

back to our house.

**8.**

*Fusion requires protons to enter the atomic nucleus.*
*This is difficult because protons all carry similar electrical charges.*
*They repel each other. Two as close as they must be*
*inside an atom repel each other with a force of about forty pounds.*

Of the Adam
of blood and bones, of
matted fur stuck
       to sticks, of the warm
air rose off the compost heap,
of the copper air
       wafted from sewers—

of the city of the rusted man-
hole, of the taste of pennies on the tongue

of the street
where they pave the front lawns
       *(you won't have to cut the grass!)*

of the cat—
       food fish gut cannery
clogging the drains

in the summer the stench climbs the hills,
wilts the roses
              on the roof—
              on the roof
of a mouth,
       a single layer of steel, thin blades
in a row, a face now smooth
as an engineered pheromone

as the grey-white steam
that billows in plumes
from the factory vents—

as a cloud,
 as a click
of hard shoes on laminate floor,
 as the click of a pen.

Adam            Atom
Fish            Fish

—the moonstones have slipped
from my eyes, but the
memory's still obscured.

**9.**

*So it is evident that a proton has to be travelling at terrific speed*
*to pass through this resistance. That is why*
*fusion won't start until the temperature is a million or more degrees.*
*The heat gives the protons the speed needed to enter the nuclei.*

In the years before I was born
I see Grandmother's
house. I see Grandmother's
kitchen: a yellow floor
divided into bricks.

                An electric
stove. Two women, long dead,
whose names my children
carry.

An aluminum lid rattles
on a pot. Grandmother sits
at the table, a pile
of pennies, a stack
of playing cards, hair
sprayed in a shell
above her head.

Two cigarettes in an ashtray
have burned to hollow tubes.

Sun through hand-sewn
curtains splits the smoke
hung in the room.
                On the stove, the cooker
is hissing, is hopping. Its gauge
pushes toward the right.

A mad tapping begins
on the stove top. It's echoed
in thunder.
                Grandmother stops—

at the highest point in the city,
all storms bring a threat
of lightning.
                        When it rains,
                the appliances are lined up
in a dark hallway, the children
are hastily unplugged.
                When it strikes—

**10.**

> *To start the fusion it is only necessary to pack the heavy forms*
> *of hydrogen around an A-bomb, whose initial temperatures*
> *reach a hundred million degrees.*

A ball of fire shoots
       across the kitchen and explodes.
Smoke from burnt metal
rises in plumes.

       Grandfather appears
in a rubber jacket, reflectors
smudged with soot, scuffed boots
with thick soles. He swings a pickaxe,
totes a hose. He douses what's left.
       Grandmother checks the stove.

All who lived
in the house are long dead.
       We push their stories
through our lips
till we mistake them
for our own,
              bear children
with anachronistic faces,
troubled movements
in their bones.

11.

> *The next step is the great puzzle. How to keep
> the hydrogen atoms from being blown apart by the A-bomb
> before they have time to fuse. To do this they must be packed
> inside some sort of case. There is nothing in creation
> that will not instantly vaporize in atom bomb heat.*

It's the night of the year's first frost.
One daughter is sleeping. The other
is still awake.

    Adam Fish,
I don't know why I've kept going back
    to this celluloid loop of memory
that isn't my own,
to a house
    that's been out of the family for years.

I've been as much
a ghost myself as dead
relatives pacing the halls in a house that belongs
to strangers

    (who paint the kitchen an awful shade of blue,
    who whitewash the smoke stained ceilings, who fill in
        the clamboil pits by the flowering quince, cover up
        the garden with a spray-on lawn, chase me out
        of the back yard when they find me
        staring at the clothesline in the middle of the night)

Remind me that memory inhabits
    a moveable place, an unfixed space,
      the peripatetic air circling the top of the water tower,
blowing over the cap
    at Sullivan's ledge, past the dredging
on the banks of the Acushnet river, up the hill

to seek me out in the attic
of a rented bungalow,

one town east.

**12.**

> *The solution may lie in delaying the melting of the bomb case*
> *for even a few billionths of a second, an interval that may permit*
> *the fast-acting forms of heavy hydrogen, deuterium, and tritium*
> *to fuse into helium.*

Atom Fish, you speak of solutions, delay.

I've lived my whole life at sea level. The salt
heat under my skin's tinged
with oil slick from the lightship
that rolled over
     in the harbor and sank. I've been stuck

  in your fractions of seconds
for years, from the slate/
  brick patio fled in my teens
  to the holes of the homes where I carved out
  innumerable lives, the gutted frames where I lived, stumbling up cobble-
stone streets to sleep it off
  with kitchen knives under the mattress, metal pots
& pans in front of the door,

  learning only I had a weak stomach
and couldn't stay awake past twelve. When I woke up,
nothing had changed.
        Atom Fish,
I have tried these solutions, none of them work.

My daughter's climbed
under her covers
but isn't asleep.

My palms are still pink,
    an upturned shell. Look close,
      the plum
wampum remembered's still there, wavy stripes
under poked-out filters,
specks of ash.

        In the back yard there's dirt
            to be dug up
              with old glass medicine bottles,
rust-etched edges of worn
Miraculous Medals, the
graces for which

I'd forgotten to ask.

**13.**

*Only the lightest-weight elements can be used for fusion.
Even in the sun no process is known for fusing anything
except hydrogen.*

Atom Fish, you speak of the things we know, you speak
of the things we don't know.
                                    I know
the hand you've been hiding's been fused
through cylinder glass. Wavy light marks the path

for your shadowed brother
who steps in while you sleep.

                I know what's on the back
of your coin, a doppelganger

without whom you're no more
than hollow, a tube of chromium steel,
worn thin enough
to float away, thin as a single layer
of an Atom

no roots, no branches, no dirt

Atom Fish, we were never alone.

**14.**

> *The A-bomb is like a match because it is started with hardly any heat. It is started by neutrons, which split atoms. These neutrons have no electrical charges. Hence, they can enter atoms without hindrance.*

It begins not in death, but in sleep.

With the Adam of blood and dirt
whose veins are of bark and of pith.

With the Adam whose tongue formed words
of a speech we forgot but we still understand.

With the Adam who buried himself
in a hole, whose flesh was devoured by

worms, whose blood
the clouds sucked up, returned
to the ocean in drops.

Whose bones resorbed into soil, deeper still
into rock, into magma, reborn in the taste

of copper pennies, piles
of metal pots and pans, a medal's

rusted edge, a counter
top, a golden chalice, waves
of liquid,
        mercury sloshed
in the gut of a fish.

**15.**

> *Neutrons as cool as the room in which you read this*
> *can and do split atoms. But the only atoms which will split*
> *with these neutrons are the very heaviest, namely*
> *plutonium and two forms of uranium.*

So sleep

anchored to the stretch of land
where our brother
climbed out of the sea
and sprung to life on a pile
of stones and wood

out of which he built the city
and its ships.

**16.**

> *These facts limit nuclear bombs to two types, A and H.*
> *No others are in sight. In fact, competent scientists*
> *figure there may never be any others. There is a definite limit*
> *to the power of an A-bomb. But there is no apparent limit*
> *to an H-bomb.*

Adam　　　　　　you were born
　　　　Fish　　of these odd combinations,
Atom　　　　　　　　born

in the yellow orb of nuclear fusion, which
travels light years to pass through the window
downstairs, beyond distance, through time to

the grandmothers, years
dead and dying, to the daughters
who carry their names,

who open their sleepy brown eyes, follow
me down to the shore, pull
identical hands from my fingers, run out

to the drift line, gather quahog shells
and bits of tumbled sea glass
from the sand.

\*

　　　　Gray gulls caw and scatter,
terns plummet from the sky,
　　　　　　　　　diving for fish
in the spaces

　　　　　　between the waves.

## ABOUT THE AUTHOR

Maggie Cleveland lives in Providence, Rhode Island, and works as a writer for the Elevator Industry Work Preservation Fund. Her poems have been featured in a number of journals and anthologies. *Atom Fish*, a chapbook, was published by One Time Press (New London, CT) in 2012. She received an MFA in creative writing from Goddard College, and is a member of the International Union of Elevator Constructors Local 7 (Baltimore) and the National Writers Union (Boston).

## ACKNOWLEDGEMENTS

Thanks first to Cobalt Press for believing in this project through a global pandemic, multiple geographical relocations, and a fuckload of revisions.

Much thanks to the teachers and mentors I've had, including: Douglas A. Martin, Kenny Fries, and Michael Klein, who taught me how to assemble a book from a stack of variegated writing experiments; John Landry, who brought me to readings, encouraged me to submit work to small journals, introduced me to poets across the country, and gave me hundreds thousands of books; Everett Hoagland, who provided guidance and encouraged my work; all of the faculty and visiting artists I attended workshops with at Goddard College through their MFA program and Clockhouse Writers' Conference; Kathryn Kulpa and members of the Somerset writing group, whose feedback and support helped shape these poems in their early stages of development; Jeanne Grandchamp and Allen Powers at Bristol Community College, who saw me as a real writer when I was young, disorganized, and completely unsure of myself; Ben Baker, who hired me to sell books and run poetry readings at his wonderful bookstore; Ira Cohen, who once gave me a key to his so I could have a place to read and write alone after hours; Tom Weigel, Jake St. John, and Jaime Duquette from the New London School of Poetry; Wikipedia, before which my poems were far less technically informed; and my Brothers and Sisters in the International Union of Elevator Constructors, without whom this book would be not nearly as electric.

And thanks most of all to my daughters, Summer and Lily, who brought forth in me the love and discipline required to write poems.

# PUBLICATION CREDITS

All of the poems in the "Elevatrix" section were assembled as cut-ups from the 2010 version of the apprenticeship curriculum of the National Elevator Industry Educational Program (NEIEP).

"The Machinery of Panic," "The Machinery of Beginnings," "The Machinery of Wantonness," "The Machinery of Surprise," and "The Machinery of God Helping Those Who Help Themselves," *DEVOURING THE GREEN: Fear of a Human Planet (a cyborg / eco poetry anthology)*. Jaded Ibis Press (Seattle, WA), 2015.

"The Machinery of Apology" was featured on the website MassPoetry.org (a foundation supporting the Massachusetts Poetry Festival) as part of the Poem of the Moment, 2014.

"The Machinery of Apology", *BURP #10*, April, 2013.

"Things I Have Learned About Elevators," *Fell Swoop #134.6*, October 2014.

"Things I have Learned About Elevators," WCAI Poetry Sunday Series, 2016.

"Things I Have Learned About Elevators (need)" and "Out from Coastal Fog," *Elephant* (New London, CT), 2016.

"Reports of Incidents" was sourced from *Public Documents of Massachusetts: Being the Annual Reports of Various Public Officers and Institutions, Vol. 10*. United States: State Printers, 1896.

"I didn't realize you were gone," WCAI Poetry Sunday Series, 2018.

"Razing the Mills", *Amerarcana: A Bird & Beckett Review*, January 2010.

"Razing the Mills," *Prevailing Wind*, Spring 2012.

"On Melancholy & the Mystery of a Street" and "Overwintering," *Cape Cod Poetry Review*, 2015.

"All of the Birds in Vermont," WCAI Poetry Sunday Series, 2020.

"Before mid-morning slides to early afternoon," *New England Poetry Club Prize Winners' Anthology*, Fall 2022.

"The blood around my heart," WCAI Poetry Sunday Series, 2021.

"Sing at the Table," *BURP #12*, 2014.

"Penumbra," *Spoonful: A Gathering of Stone Soup Poets*, December 2012.

"we largely involve the enormous", *Elephant* (New London, CT), January 2010.

*Atom Fish*, chapbook, One Time Press (New London, CT), November 2012.

"Atom Fish: Prologue," "Atom Fish: I," "Atom Fish: II," "Atom Fish: III," "Atom Fish: IV," The Offending Adam (http://theoffendingadam.com/), 2012.

"Atom Fish" used the following source text: Blakeslee, Howard W. "Atom 'Fish,' of Changing Weight, Make H-Bomb." *Milwaukee Sentinel 18 Aug 1950, Section 1:4.* Print.

www.ingramcontent.com/pod-product-compliance
Lightning Source LLC
Chambersburg PA
CBHW061809070526
44586CB00024B/2780